HELLO Faith

SANDRA F. HOLT

www.TrueVinePublishing.org

Hello Faith
Sandra F. Holt

Published by True Vine Publishing Co.
810 Dominican Dr. Ste 103
Nashville, TN 37228
www.TrueVinePublishing.org

Copyright © 2024 by Sandra Holt: All rights reserved. No part of this book may be reproduced in any form or by any electronic or mechanical means, including information storage and retrieval or mechanical means without permission in writing from the publisher, except by a reviewer who may quote brief passages in a review.

ISBN: 978-1-962783-18-7 Paperback
ISBN: 978-1-962783-19-4 eBook

Scripture taken from the Holy Bible, King James version unless otherwise noted.

"Scripture quotations taken from the Amplified® Bible (AMP), Copyright © 2015 by The Lockman Foundation. Used by permission. lockman.org"

Scripture quotations taken from The Holy Bible, New International Version® NIV® Copyright © 1973, 1978, 1984, 2011 by Biblica, Inc. Used with permission. All rights reserved worldwide.

Scripture quotations marked (TLB) are taken from The Living Bible, copyright © 1971 by Tyndale House Foundation. Used by permission of Tyndale House Publishers, Carol Stream, Illinois 60188. All rights reserved.

Scripture quotations marked (CEV) are from the Contemporary English Version Copyright © 1991, 1992, 1995 by American Bible Society. Used by Permission.

Printed in the United States—first printing

Dedication

This book is dedicated in loving memory of my parents Leonard McGhee Sr. and Anna McGhee plus my beloved oldest sister Lynell McGhee Hamilton. I also dedicate this book to my family and friends along with my prayer group, Women of Purpose, as they all partook in hearing sections of the manuscript prior to its completion. I believe this book contains valuable keys that will ignite our faith as it takes us on a journey of reflection, growth and healing.

Table of Contents

Preface

In writing my book *Goodbye Fear,* I, through inspiration from God, encouraged readers to let fear go as I provided Biblical principles in addressing fear. Isn't it just like God to tell me to not stop there. If we are to say goodbye to fear, it is only befitting that we say hello to something that is worthwhile and life changing. I believe that's why God led me to write the book *Hello Faith.*

In fact, my book *Goodbye Fear* is incomplete without *Hello Faith.* The beginning of the book starts off with a letter to "Faith" and ends with a revised letter to "Faith" where I personify faith in order for the reader to come to see how valuable faith is to our lives. When we embrace faith, we are embracing God's promises and by embracing God's promises, we are expecting a response back or something in return as we utilize our faith. It is time to truly acknowledge the importance of faith or faith in God's Word.

What better way to start your day or even morning than with *Hello Faith.* Faith is one of the main weapons we are to use to deal with every attack by the enemy. Faith is the power force behind obtaining anything you are believing God for. The word "Hello" alone can change the mood or atmosphere of a situation as it is welcoming and inviting.

Add faith to that and your day is complete. I Corin-

Sandra F. Holt

thians 13:13 (New King James Version) "And now abide faith, hope, love, these three; but the greatest of these is love." There are prerequisites as to what a Christian should live by, and faith is a profound prerequisite. We must come to see that to live a prosperous life faith must be part of the ingredient. My prayer is that by the end of this book faith will illuminate in your heart, that faith will come so alive that you will realize, "You can't make one move without her." My prayer is that you will see a life unimaginable without faith and proclaim each day. "Hello Faith."

A Letter to Faith

Hello Faith,

I realize I have not talked with You in a while. I just wanted to let You know that no major accomplishments or even miracles appear to have occurred in my life since You have been absent. Hope has been at my door, but You, Faith, have not been present as I continuously failed to extend the invitation. I wanted to invite You, but I regretfully kept inviting some of Your enemies.

You know the main ones: Fear, Doubt and yes, Unbelief. I invited them, and they showed up eagerly each day in my life focusing on negative things that brought me no peace. In fact, they worked in harmony and attacked my hopes and dreams. My mind was bombarded with everything they were saying to me and because I uninvited You, I believed them.

I believed their lies regarding my health, my family, my finances and that God's promises were not for me. You can only imagine how miserable life has been without Your presence in my life. It has been truly hard. It is only by the grace of God that I am still here. Many times, I wanted to give up. The more I allowed Your enemies to show up, the more I was blind to what a wonderful difference You had once made in my life.

As they showed up, You became more and more distant to me. It actually came to a point that I had to ques-

Sandra F. Holt

tion whether I ever knew You. My life is so empty without You, and I am so miserable with this void in my life. I am literally at my wits end. I so desperately need You back in my life.

Having You in my life made a positive difference. It is beyond me why I ever let You go. My dreams ultimately have been left unfulfilled and most of all, I have been unable to please my loving Father God without You. How do I get You back in my life? I am at a crossroad, and I need help.

***

Can you relate to this letter to Faith? If we are truly honest, I believe many can relate to this letter. Have you ever found yourself uninviting faith in your life? For some of you, you may ask how do I uninvite faith?

Do you ever stress over situations or lay awake worried? If the answer is yes, then those are signs that faith was uninvited. I believe this letter addresses what happens when we fail to have faith. We need faith to know that situations in our lives can change for the better.

We need faith to know that our bodies can be healed. We need faith to know that things can and will work out. As you walk down memory lane regarding your life, what would be your responses to the following questions?

- What has caused you to walk in unbelief when you have the promises from God?
- Have you ever questioned whether the promises

10

in God's Word are for you?

- What has caused you to be in constant worry over a situation or circumstance?
- Has faith been evident in your life? And is faith evident now?

I wrote this simple letter to Faith because I realize now more than ever that the way we rise above fear, doubt and unbelief is to exercise our faith. We must come to see beyond a doubt that to get major things accomplished in our lives, faith's presence is a must! As you read this book, my prayer is that you will awaken to the importance of having faith in your life. May your heart and mind be enlightened.

May God grant you wisdom to realize that the answers that you need are produced through faith as it is awakened inside of you. Are you **"FAITH IS READY TO HELP US OVERCOME AND BE VICTORIOUS."** ready to embrace each day knowing the necessity of faith? Why not start today? Why not start now? Let's welcome faith together!

May *Hello Faith* become a constant reminder of the value faith plays in our lives every day. As we utilize our faith over issues and concerns, we are constantly developing our faith. Faith is ready to help us overcome and be victorious. What is going on in your life right now?

God wants faith to be made perfect in you. I remember a minister preached a sermon "Make Christ perfect in

11

you" when I was in college years ago. That message still impacts my life today. Although I am not perfect, I desire Christ to be perfected in me, meaning God's direction for my life. God wants us to get to the point that when we utilize our faith, we know it is already done which is evident that Christ is being perfected in us. In essence, faith in God gets results. Faith in God gets it done!

So, What is Faith?

To ensure we exercise faith in our daily lives, we need to be able to define faith. I believe in the simplest form faith is trusting God's Word. Faith is not an emotion. It is not a feeling. It is a spiritual fact that what God has promised He is able and will accomplish.

Hebrews 11:1 states, "Now faith is the substance of things hoped for, the evidence of things not seen." I believe that it is imperative that we meditate on what this scripture says. Think about it. Faith is the assurance that we will receive those things we are believing God for.

> "FAITH IS BELIEVING WHAT GOD SAYS ABOUT YOU, YOUR FAMILY, AND EVERY CONDITION IN YOUR LIFE."

In essence, faith is believing what God says about you, your family, and every condition in your life. Faith is complete trust and dependence on God. The Word says that God is a Spirit and they that worship Him must worship Him in spirit and in truth. So, if God is a Spirit and God requires us to walk by faith and not by sight then faith is a spiritual law set in motion by God.

Regardless of your situation or circumstance, you can rest in God's perfect peace knowing that He is working every situation out for you. I don't know what you are dealing with right now, but I encourage you to trust God at His Word. 2 Corinthians 1:20 states, "For all the promises of God in Him are Yes, and in Him Amen, to the glory of God through us." When we know God's promises then faith assures us that they are ours for the asking, and for the receiving.

God desires us to put our total trust in Him according to Proverbs 3:6 which states, "Trust in the LORD with all thine heart; and lean not unto thine own understanding." It is not for us to wonder how things will work out. It is for us to know that things will work out. Proverbs 3 further tells us that in all our ways acknowledge Him and He will direct our paths. It is comforting to know that as we acknowledge God in every situation and circumstance in our lives, He will surely direct our paths as we put our ultimate faith in Him.

If we want to please God, then faith is a key ingredient. To obtain anything from God, we must operate in faith. The Word states that he that comes to God must believe that He is God and He is a rewarder of them that diligently seek Him.

Let's look at Hebrews 11:1 (Amplified).

"Now faith is the <u>assurance</u> (title deed, confirmation) of things hoped for (divinely guaranteed), and the <u>evidence</u> of things not seen [the conviction of their reality—faith comprehends as fact what cannot be experienced by the physical senses]."

This is powerful! Faith is your assurance. Faith is

your title deed. When you own faith, faith owns you. Faith is your reality beyond the senses.

Have you ever ordered products from places like Amazon? I am a regular customer of Amazon. When I order from Amazon, I do not immediately receive the product(s) but what I do immediately receive is my confirmation that the product has been purchased and is on its way. I don't stress over it or worry whether the product is coming. Why? Because I have the confirmation. Well guess what?

Faith is your confirmation. You may not immediately see the physical evidence of what you are believing for, but faith lets you know that your request to God is received. You have the confirmation from God's Word. It's on its way.

"FAITH...IS BASED ON WHAT YOU CAN SPIRITUALLY SEE WHICH IS DIVINELY GUARANTEED."

Again, faith is not based on what you can physically see but faith is based on the promises of God. In essence, it is what you can spiritually see. I repeat, it is based on what you can spiritually see which is divinely guaranteed.

Have you ever just known things were going to work out although you didn't see the physical evidence? Guess what? That is faith in action. Who makes the guarantee? God does. Hope plays a role, but it is faith that gets results. It is a divine guarantee that what you are believing God for will materialize.

Sandra F. Holt

What happens when you pay your house off? You get the title deed. A title deed is a legal deed or document constituting evidence of a right, especially ownership of property. Faith is your title deed. It gives you the rights to all the promises of God.

Faith serves as your spiritual eyes like your physical eyes serve in the natural. That is why faith doesn't wait on your physical eyes to see the materialization because faith sees it before the physical manifestation.

> "NOT ONLY IS FAITH YOUR EYES IN THE SPIRIT, BUT FAITH HAS A VOICE."

Not only is faith your eyes in the spirit, but faith has a voice. Faith speaks. God said let there be light. So, when was there light? When God spoke it. God's Words completed the declaration when light appeared. When God said let there be, that settled it. It was done. Faith says it's done.

Martin Luther King Jr. said, "Faith is taking the first step, even when you don't see the whole staircase." We don't have to see the whole staircase because faith says it is there and by taking that first step, you are acting on your faith.

Imagine getting ready to drive to an exciting destination; while driving you can only see so far with your physical eyes but not seeing the entire distance does not deter you from making the trip. Although you can only see so far down the road, you trust your aptitude to make it to the destination, regardless of the distractions along life's highways. Faith knows that if you trust and believe

16

God you will receive and get to your journey's end. Faith says you will arrive.

Maybe all you have right now is a promise from God. I assure you that's enough to keep driving, to keep moving. While driving, you may see a stopped car, an ambulance, or road construction. None of these diversions stop you from driving. Occasionally you may see a state trooper; if speeding, that may cause you to slow down but it does not cause you to stop. You may even be rerouted to go a different way, but you continue to focus on your destination. That is the same with faith. There may be

"FAITH IS NOW!"

distractions along the way and maybe even disappointments, but God does not want us to be distracted and stop moving. He wants us to keep the faith. There are trials and tribulations in this life as Jesus said but He said to be of good cheer as He has overcome every obstacle that we face.

Hebrew 11:1 also has a powerful Word that we can miss if we read too fast. It states, "**Now** Faith..." Faith is current. Faith is present. Faith is NOW! What are you believing God for? Then take it NOW. What do you want to see manifested in your life and in the lives of those you love? Take it NOW.

There are no limitations when we put our trust in God. God is calling us to have the mind of Christ. Christ

17

did not see any impossibilities. He only saw possibilities. We must believe and take God at His Word. In fact, the scriptures tell us that He is not a man that He should lie nor the Son of Man that He should repent. If God said it, it is so.

Faith opens our minds to the things of God. That is what faith does. That is what faith says. That is what faith is.

I remember as a little girl, there was a misunderstanding with a neighbor's child next door. I had my version of the story and the neighbor's child had another version. When I tried to explain my version to my neighbor's parent, the neighbor's parent replied, "I don't want to hear it." That has stayed with me all these years. Why? Because the neighbor believed what their child was saying. As far as my neighbor was concerned, I had no validity.

If we are walking in the light of God's Word, we should not want to hear any voice that is not God's voice. Why? Because we have His ear, and He should have ours. What does God want us to say when Satan comes with his lies and deception? I believe God wants us to say, "I don't want to hear it." You know what? That's faith! Why? Because faith only hears and believes the voice of God's Word.

My older sister and brother often told me about times when I was a little girl, and I wanted one specific pacifier that I often would lose. They said I would throw a temper tantrum wanting everyone to join me in finding it. That seems hard to believe but I will keep going. The point is that I wanted it NOW.

In other words, I did not give up in the search nor did I allow anyone else give up in the search until my pacifier was found. I was told many times that I would be the one to find the pacifier, because in essence, I knew where it was all along.

If we know God's Word is true and He is faithful, then we must not give up because faith sees it already done. Faith says you already have it. Faith doesn't ever give up because faith in God is focusing on the NOW and not the HOW. Now Faith! It is present in God's presence. Can you say? "Hello Faith, I am believing for the impossible." I will say it, "Hello Faith, I am believing for the impossible!"

I like the song "Victory" by Brenda Waters. The lyrics state in part,

"I don't know how God's gonna do it. I don't know when, when He's gonna fix it...I only know. Yes. God's gonna make a way for me... You can help me sing (victory). Listen. He never told me how He's gonna (do it)..."

This song is so powerful to me. Why? Because it demonstrates faith in action. We may not know how God is going to work a situation out, but faith assures us that He will work it out. We can use our faith to claim victory over our family, our friends, our dreams, and our health

Sandra F. Holt

by proclaiming God's Word.

The Bible also teaches us that we have the victory. "For everyone born of God overcomes the world. This is the victory that has overcome the world, even our faith." (1 John 5:4, NIV). Whatever you are believing God for, I encourage you to hold on to it. It will become visible. Faith brings the unseen into the seen. Faith says you can do all things through Christ which strengthens you. Faith says that what you desire is yours for the asking and believing.

"FAITH TAKES THE 'IM' OUT OF IMPOSSIBLE." Faith doesn't focus on the condition. Faith stands on the Word of God. Faith takes the can't out of the equation and turns it into can. Faith takes the "im" out of impossibilities and leaves only possibilities. Faith supercharges our lives as we focus on the promises of God.

I think about the woman in the Bible with the issue of blood. The scripture states that she had suffered many things of many physicians. She had spent all her money trying to get better but she was only getting worse. When she heard of Jesus, she believed that He was a healer. She believed that He could change her situation and heal her body. She said, "If I may touch but his clothes, I shall be whole." She simply believed. Her faith gave her the strength to not give up.

No doubt her body was physically weak trying to get to Jesus but that did not stop her. God does not want us to give up. The woman could have looked at her situation and gave up, but she didn't. She refused to allow her physical weakness to stand in the way of her miracle. Could it be we often times allow our physical weakness to stand in the way of our miracle? We can learn from the woman with the issue of blood that focused on getting to Jesus.

She possibly had to ignore negative thoughts that bombarded her mind, but she kept her hope and believed by faith that her situation would turn around. She used her faith to get to Jesus and she used her faith to get her healing. She knew that no one could help her other than Jesus. When we truly realize that the answer is in Jesus, faith gets us what we need.

So, what happened? She got to Jesus and touched the helm of His garment and immediately she was healed. Jesus' response was, "Who touched me?" When your faith is in action, the Lord of Lord and King of Kings will say, "Who touched me?" That's what faith does – Touches God and moves God.

We can't give up. Faith is powerful. Faith is fulfilling. Faith works with hope. Faith brings peace. Faith is NOW!

I remember once swiping my credit card and it declined. When the card declined, I was baffled because I knew beyond a shadow of a doubt two things: (1) The membership on the card had been paid, and (2) I had used very little of the available credit. So, what caused the decline? I determined that I had failed to realize that

Sandra F. Holt

the expiration date on the card had expired, and I had been sent a new one to activate.

Could it be that we don't see the manifestations of what we are believing God for because we have not activated our faith? Has your faith expired while waiting on your blessing? When we get weary with waiting on the answer or manifestation of our miracle, we should be reminded that our membership is for life. This membership has been bought and paid for with the blood of Jesus.

"HAS YOUR FAITH EXPIRED WHILE WAITING ON YOUR BLESSING?"

We should also be reminded that blessings from God will never run out and they have no expiration date. We should additionally be reminded that just because we don't see an immediate manifestation with our physical eyes, it does not mean we have not received what we are believing for. Just like with my credit card, I knew that it was mine; I had the available credit, and the purchasing power was available to me. How much more to know when it comes to our request to God.

The blessings are ours as we activate our faith which is our purchasing power. Another word for activate is "turn on." Let's turn our faith on and keep it on in Jesus' name. We must activate our faith. Maybe right now your hope is alive, but faith is not. I heard someone say, "hope gets you in the door, but faith causes the manifestation."

See, no one could have convinced me that the credit card was not authentic and that the available credit was not there. I knew the decline was only temporary. Once I activated the credit card with the correct expiration date, I was able to use it.

As you read and prayerfully reread this book, I pray God will perform supernatural miracles in your life as all will be accomplished by faith; however, it must be activated.

Matthew 15:22-28:

"And, behold, a woman of Canaan came out of the same coasts, and cried unto him, saying, Have mercy on me, O Lord, thou son of David; my daughter is grievously vexed with a devil. But he answered her not a word. And his disciples came and besought him, saying, Send her away; for she crieth after us. But he answered and said, I am not sent but unto the lost sheep of the house of Israel.

Then came she and worshipped him, saying, Lord, help me. But he answered and said, It is not meet to take the children's bread, and to cast it to dogs. And she said, Truth, Lord: yet the dogs eat of the crumbs which fall from their masters' table. Then Jesus answered and said unto her, O woman, great is thy faith: be it unto thee even as thou wilt. And her daughter was made whole from that very hour."

Sandra F. Holt

This is one of my favorite stories in the Bible. It is a powerful story watching the woman's faith in action. Why is this so powerful? For you Bible readers, you know that Jesus first came to the children of Israel or the Jews to heal, deliver and set them free. This woman was not a Jew. She was a Gentile. But because she had faith, it did not matter. Faith trumps everything. The woman's faith caused her to claim her daughter's healing out of the future and brought it into the present.

Why do I say her faith brought her miracle out of the future into the present? Because it was predestined for salvation and deliverance to come to the Gentiles after being offered to the Jews; however, for this woman, it did not matter that she was a Gentile, her faith got her the results she desired.

Galatians tells us that there is no longer Jews or Gentiles as we are all one in Christ Jesus. This story displays a beautiful scenery of what faith can and will do. Again, Faith is Now!

When we hear stories of men and women who overcame immeasurable odds, we should be encouraged that we can overcome as well. Many times, our own testimonies are the conduit for someone else's deliverance. People are looking for others who have had similar experiences that overcame overwhelming odds.

Some may say, "I can believe for everyone else but myself." I believe this is a sincere statement, but it is easier to exercise faith when you are not in the storm and when it is not your specific dream to be realized. There are many areas in my life where Gods has delivered me and set me free, and I came out of my struggles victoriously. I try to be understanding of other people who are struggling to exercise their faith because I was once in their shoes. Hebrews 4:15(AMP) states,

"For we do not have a High Priest who is unable to sympathize and understand our weaknesses and temptations, but One who has been tempted [knowing exactly how it feels to be human] in every respect as we are, yet without [committing any] sin."

Jesus went through the same trials as mankind. He understands and has compassion for others and so should we. I don't expect my children to possess some of the wisdom that I have right now, although I am not saying wisdom is age specific. But there should be an expectation that we grow in the knowledge of God as believers. These personal testimonies where people overcame challenging times are ones that I give the greatest weight to.

When David told Saul he would fight Goliath, it was because he had already faced a lion and a bear. He knew what God could and would do. David's prior experience with the lion and the bear already had his faith super charged when the situation with Goliath came along.

See, when we have faith in God's Word to get through any situation and we stand on that, then and only

Sandra F. Holt

then does our test become a testimony. In each of our testimonies where we stood on God's Word, the one ingredient that we all share is faith. God tells believers to believe Him and trust Him. He wants us to be that tree planted by the rivers of water. That tree may bend but it will not break.

The only break we should partake in is a faith outbreak. What if there was a faith outbreak where we denounce everything that does not line up with God's Word? If you are on a journey with God, you are destined to succeed. The scripture states that they that wait on the Lord shall renew their strength. We must wait on the Lord and be encouraged.

> "THE ONLY BREAK WE SHOULD PARTAKE IN IS A FAITH OUTBREAK."

Faith reminds us that we are winners because we are on the winning team. Faith is constantly focusing on the plans of God. We must continuously decide that we are no longer going to listen to the lies of the enemy. NO! God says my sheep hear my voice and a stranger they will not follow. Faith listens to the voice of God and while we listen, we follow.

God wants us to know the power of faith and the unlimited blessings that are ours when we exercise our faith. However, Satan does not want us to know the power of trusting and believing God's Word. When faith has settled in our hearts, we shouldn't see obstacles; we should see opportunities. We shouldn't see the problem; we should see the problem solver. We shouldn't see lack;

we should see more than enough.

You see, faith should change how we see things. As long as Satan can keep us looking at our circumstance with the mind of doom and gloom, we cannot receive all God desires for us. What are you looking at right now? What are you seeing? Are you in need of a faith adjustment? Adjust your faith to see what God wants for you. Adjust your faith today.

Sandra F. Holt

Take time to list your desires before God. Declare to God that you are taking His precious promises today by faith and that is victory!

Lord I am believing you for and I take it by faith...

_____

_____

_____

_____

_____

_____

_____

_____

_____

_____

_____

_____

_____

_____

_____

_____

_____

Living by Faith

Have you really thought about what it means to live by faith; or what it means to walk by faith and not by sight? To live by faith is to make God's Word your life. It is realizing that you cannot live absent from faith. That is what I have come to see. I believe that is what many men and women in the Bible who operated in great faith came to see.

On that Damascus Road, Paul's life was miraculously changed. Through the Spirit of God, Paul came to see that to live is Christ and to die is gain; meaning while he was alive, everything was about fulfilling God's purpose for his life. Paul embraced faith as he embraced and accepted the son of God, Jesus Christ.

Romans 12:3 tells us that God has given every man the measure of faith. So, what do we need to do? We need to exercise our faith or live by faith. We need to spend time in God's Word. How can we know God's promises unless we read them in His Word?

Habakkuk 2:4, states in part, *"...but the just shall live by his faith."* This is a familiar scripture for most Christians. When we live by faith, we are acceptable to God. We must put our faith in the one and only true God.

Even in the natural, we exhibit faith. When we turn our stove on to cook, we believe that the stove will work. When we sit in a chair, we don't stop to examine it.

When we get into our cars to go someplace, we grab the keys and go without thinking twice about whether or not the car will start. These are examples of natural faith.

If we can trust man's inventions, we must learn to trust God who made man. For believers, God said that we are in this world but not of this world. This world has a system for us to use money to purchase or get what we want. God has a heavenly system and His system embodies faith.

"IF WE CAN TRUST MAN'S INVENTIONS, WE MUST LEARN TO TRUST GOD WHO MADE MAN."

Romans 8:24 states, "For we are saved by hope: but hope that is seen is not hope: for what a man seeth, why doth he yet hope for?" Hope plays an important role. Hope is the desire to receive something. If you don't have the desire, you won't go to the next step of believing for the materialization which is faith. In living by faith, there must be a desire. Once the desire takes place, it becomes possible when faith is exercised.

Hebrews 11:6 states, "But without faith it is impossible to please him: for he that cometh to God must believe that he is, and that he is a rewarder of them that diligently seek him." You see we cannot please God without the faith ingredient. There are no exceptions. Living by faith is a must in everything we say and do.

God is calling every believer in Christ to live a life of faith. The Bible states God rewards us when we sincerely search for Him. Are you diligently seeking God?

If so, then get ready to be rewarded for He delights to give His children good things. Everywhere we go and everything we do should demonstrate our faith.

As we live by faith, we come to see that faith is the currency in a Christian's world. How do we live by faith? By saying what God says. Faith is God's language and anything else is a break in communication.

If I go to a country that does not speak English, then it will be difficult for me to survive unless I have an interpreter. When we have the faith that God will do just what He said, then we don't have to worry about needing an interpreter as we understand the language of God because God's Spirit lives in every believer.

Ephesians 6:11 states, "Put on the whole armor of God, that we may be able to stand against the wiles of the devil." Guess what is part of the armor of God? I believe you guessed it. It is faith.

Ephesians 6:16 states, "Above all, taking the shield of faith, wherewith ye shall be able to quench all the fiery darts of the wicked." If God has given us the armor then we should know that we are assured to win every attack the devil brings our way; being fully persuaded that we should not allow our circumstance to silence our faith. We must use our faith to silence our circumstances. God is calling us to live the life where we recognize faith as being a part of our daily armor. God wants us to embrace faith and wear the armor according to His Word.

In Proverbs 4, the Word of God talks about wisdom,

Sandra F. Holt

understanding, and the importance it plays in our lives. Proverbs 4:5-6 states, "Get wisdom, get understanding: forget it not; neither decline from the words of my mouth. Forsake her not, and she shall preserve thee: love her, and she shall keep thee." Here God is revealing to us the person of wisdom and how wisdom will keep us.

I believe God wants us to personify faith. What does that mean? Embrace faith as if you cannot survive without her. Embody faith as if you cannot survive without her. Proclaim faith as if you cannot survive without her, and live faith as if you cannot survive without her.

Romans 1:17 states in part, "...The just shall live by faith." Who are the just? Those who have right standing with God. Those who have accepted Jesus into their lives.

Each day, as we are living a life of faith, we rest in the confidence of the goodness of God. Romans 8:28 states, "And we know that all things work together for good to them that love God, to them who are the called according to his purpose." Living a life of faith reminds us that we live a life where God's mercies are new every morning and great is his faithfulness.

CeCe Winans sings *Goodness of God* which is so powerful. The lyrics state that His goodness is chasing after us. God wants the best for us. He came that we may have life and have it more abundantly. He wants us to live a fulfilled, enriched life. That's God's goodness on our lives. That's God's goodness chasing after us.

While taking road trips and leaving one state and approaching another, we often see a Welcome sign. We can also apply that to our lives spiritually when we leave the ways of the world and enter God's kingdom. God says, "Welcome." I believe God is saying, "Welcome to the Kingdom of God where faith is our currency."

To operate by faith, we must operate in the Kingdom of God. What is the Kingdom of God? It is the place where God rules. For believers, it exists within us.

It is a changed mindset where Jesus has Lordship over our lives. Mark 4:30-32 (TLB) states,

"How can I describe the Kingdom of God? What story should I use to illustrate it? It is like a mustard seed planted in the ground. It is the smallest of all seeds, but it becomes the largest of all garden plants; it grows long branches, and birds can make nests in its shade."

The Kingdom of God grows and He desires every believer to play an active role in His Kingdom where He rules. That is why we are in this world as believers but not of this world. As part of the Kingdom of God, we receive our instructions where God says, use your currency called faith for whatever you are standing in the need of in this life.

See, nothing can stop the Kingdom of God from growing and nothing can stop your faith from producing the results you desire. So, let's move and grow in the

Sandra F. Holt

name of the Lord. When I was a little girl, there were two sitcoms that I enjoyed watching: "I Dream of Jeannie" and "Bewitched." Why? Because on the show, "I Dream of Jeannie" all Jeannie needed to do was to nod her head and whatever she wanted happened. In "Bewitched" all Samantha needed to do was to wiggle her nose and whatever she wanted occurred. I am not encouraging or mindful of magic, but it is the fixation that whatever they wanted, it was theirs.

Guess what. We don't need magic. All we need is faith. All we need is God. We have a faith ATM (Automatic to Me) Card activated to us. Let God activate those blessings you are believing Him for. Faith makes it happen. Are you ready to walk down faith lane and take all the promises God has for you?

Faith removes all limitations for you to have an unlimited supply with God. We should all strive to allow God's Word to become greater and greater in each of us. As this happens, it becomes a constant reminder that there are no restrictions in God.

I like the way T.D. Jakes says it, "Get Ready, Get Ready, Get Ready." What type of mindset do you have when you go on family vacations? Do you see the world a little differently? What about those problems? Many times, when on family vacations, I find myself in a different mindset, in a good way. The excitement and time on the trip seem to override everything.

As a grandmother, it is extremely fun watching my grandchildren enjoy themselves. What if we consciously took vacations or faith trips in our lives every day? I believe we would see things from a different perspective. We would have no worry and no anxiety because we are on a faith trip. Again, Jesus said the just shall live by faith. Well, the only way we can live by faith is to stay continuously on a faith trip using our faith map and traveling to all the destinations God plans for us.

Imagine what would happen if we were taught that all things were possible from birth. What type of life would we have? That's what happens when we accept Jesus into our lives, we become born again and we are taught that all things are possible. We are encouraged to know that we are overcomers regardless of circumstances in our lives. That's the life God is calling us to. That is living the life of faith. That is ultimately living the good life.

I believe God is calling us to raise our level of expectation as we live by faith. When we raise our level of expectation, our faith increases. Faith moves you from the waiting line to the blessing line.

Jesus says in Mark 11:24, "Therefore I say unto you, What things soever ye desire, when ye pray, believe that ye receive them, and ye shall have them." I listened to a minister who preached this scripture and lived by it his entire life as he saw God do powerful things in his life before he went home to be with the Lord.

Sandra F. Holt

When I was in college, God allowed Luke 18 to come alive in my heart. I was believing God to open doors in my life, and I enjoyed reading the story about the widowed woman going to the unjust judge asking him to avenge her. The point that blessed me was when God said, "Hear what the unjust judge sayeth and will not God avenge His own elect..."

That is encouraging. God will avenge us in our lives. I encourage you to hold onto your faith for those prayers that you have been praying and have not seen the manifestation. Form a vision in your mind on how you want things to work out. Meditate on God's Words and promises. Use your imagination. It came from God.

"YOU CAN HAVE BIG DREAMS BECAUSE YOU HAVE A BIG GOD."

You can have big dreams because you have a big God. Will God not avenge His own elect? We must continue to trust God regardless of how uncertain things may look or seem.

What is God saying to you? What is your faith speaking? Once it gets in your heart, it is only a matter of time when your heart's desires will manifest. I remember praying with my prayer group when I heard God say, "Let them know that they have my ear." That was powerful to me. We have the ear of God. What we are believing for is possible as we live a life of faith.

When we really become aware of who we are and whose we are, we are ready to turn the world upside down. Are you ready? I am. Whatever has been holding you back, I encourage you to take charge over it and move forward by utilizing your faith. With the strength of God, know that nothing can hold you back. God has great plans for us. Let's continue to celebrate with others and believe God will open His store house of blessings for everyone who operates by faith. In fact, the more we receive, there's much more to get. What makes me know this? Faith.

Faith-Repeat

Mark 5 tells us how Jesus healed a man's daughter who had died. When Jesus showed up where she was, He told them she was not

> "WHEN WE REALLY BECOME AWARE OF WHO WE ARE AND WHOSE WE ARE, WE ARE READY TO TURN THE WORLD UPSIDE DOWN."

dead but asleep. When He said that, they began to laugh at Him. Jesus put them out of the room where the daughter was. He only allowed the child's parents and three of His disciples, one being Peter to stay in the room.

A similar scenario occurred later in Acts 9 when Peter raised a woman from the dead. Peter modeled after Jesus. He put all the doubters out of the room. Those who were crying and weeping were not allowed to stay in the room and once he put them out of the room, then Peter prayed and spoke to the woman to arise and she opened her eyes and sat up.

What was in action? Faith. Who had Peter seen demonstrate this? Jesus. You see how God wants us to use

His Word to turn things around by exercising our faith.

Peter demonstrated what he had seen and was taught. Peter was living the faith life as he impersonated Jesus. That is what we should be doing in the spiritual. Who are you impersonating? Who are you listening to?

Peter followed Jesus' example. I call this faith-repeat. It Is a constant reminder if God did it once, He surely can do it again. God wants us to participate in faith-repeat. We may have to remove ourselves from the doubters or even the emotional ties and that is okay because if we imitate Jesus, we are assured the victory living the faith life.

Hebrews 12:1 states,

"Wherefore seeing we also are compassed about with so great a cloud of witnesses... and let us run with patience the race that is set before us, Looking unto Jesus the author and finisher of our faith..."

My daddy who has gone on to be with the Lord delivered a powerful message titled: "Cloud of Witnesses" that still blesses me today. He is now a part of the cloud of witnesses cheering for those of us still on earth. Jesus tells us to run with patience the race and look to Jesus the author and finisher of our faith. This is good news. Jesus is the author and finisher of our faith (Hebrews 12:2).

Everything is centered around Jesus. He is our example from start to finish. He is our example as to how to walk by faith and not by sight. An author is the originator of the script. Jesus is the originator of the script but also the finisher. He completes us.

Colossians 1:16 states.

"For by him were all things created, that are in heaven, and that are in earth, visible and invisible, whether they be thrones, or dominions, or principalities, or powers: all things were created by him, and for him."

Jesus is our example of walking by faith. While we continue to strive to live the life Jesus' desires for us, we are still not perfected. We continue to mature as we allow Christ to lead and guide us. Knowing Jesus is the author of our faith is encouraging and knowing He is the finisher of our faith is equally encouraging as it is a constant reminder that only He can complete us.

Benefits of Faith

In my book *Goodbye Fear*, I asked the readers to look at the benefits of fear, but of course, I was being sarcastic. However, there are immeasurable benefits of faith. We must know there are no benefits of fear unless we are talking about a reverential fear of God.

Psalm 103:1-2 states, "Bless the LORD, O my soul: and all that is within me, bless his holy name. Bless the LORD, O my soul, and forget not all his benefits." Merriam-Webster defines "benefits" as something that produces good or helpful results or effects that promotes well-being.

The benefits of serving God, believing God, and honoring God truly produces good and helpful results. 3 John and 2 state, "Beloved, I wish above all things that thou mayest prosper and be in health, even as thy soul prospereth." Psalm 103 goes on to tell us that He forgives our wrong doings; he heals all our diseases; He redeems our life from destruction; He provides lovingkindness and tender mercies; He satisfies our mouth with good things, so that our youth is renewed. Wow! What benefits are available to us if we only believe and receive them by faith.

As a parent, I have always wanted the best for my children as I am sure most parents do. I encourage them to pursue their dreams and the calling on their lives.

That's what God wants for us. God wants the best for us. We are His children. He wants us to partake of all that He has to offer us.

Working on a job comes with a benefit package. Sometimes people accept a job not specifically for the pay but based on the benefits. What is a benefit package? It is the goods you get for working there. God's benefit package is the goods we get for trusting Him.

Jeremiah 1 tells us that God is watchful of His Word to perform it. We can rest with the blessed hope that when we put our trust in God's Word, He comes through every time

"FAITH PRODUCES OVERWHELMING BENEFITS FROM GOD."

for us as He looks over His Word to perform His promises.

What will get you out of that place of despair? Faith. What can get you into the overflow of God's blessings? Faith. What can open doors for you? Faith. What gets you to believe all things are possible? Faith. What can move you from hearing God's promises to seeing them manifested in your life? Faith. You get the picture?

You see the benefits of faith? God has set everything in motion to be accomplished by faith. Faith produces overwhelming benefits from God. Praise God for His Benefits!

Forever Increasing Faith

Faith is spiritual and without faith it is impossible to please God. But did you know that God desires and expects our faith to grow? If a child stays the same size from the age of one to ten, would you be concerned? God is concerned if our faith is not growing.

We are to go from faith to faith. The scripture tells us to grow in the nurture and admonition of the Lord. Think about the challenges in your life. Sometimes, during challenges in our lives, we see our faith grow.

We find ourselves reading our Bible more often as we await to hear from God, desiring Him to work a situation out in our lives. One of the things that the enemy wants us to do is get comfortable. When we get comfortable, we stop growing. We find ourselves spending very little time meditating and reading God's Word.

In my Book *Goodbye Fear,* I shared how I struggled with the fear of sickness and disease and how fear gained access into my life as a little girl. I constantly worried about my mom who was in and out of the hospital numerous times. I so desperately wanted my mom healthy like other moms.

As I grew into adulthood, I finally came to realize, through the wisdom of God, that I was operating from the soulish realm where my emotions were ruling and my faith was not being exercised. I finally came to the point of No More! No more allowing my emotions to rule! No more living in fear and anxiety! Simply No More!

To accomplish No More!, I begin to grow my faith as I focused on the promises of God. I read and meditated on God's Word to allow God's Word to get into my spirit. I came to the resolve that faith in God could overcome any obstacles or challenge in my life, including sickness and disease.

Romans 10:17 tells us, "So then faith cometh by hearing, and hearing by the word of God." This tells us that our faith grows as we continue to hear the Word of God. We must have something to hear and believe before we can exercise our faith. As you continue to hear the Word of God, it gets in your heart and when it gets in your heart you believe what faith says about you and what faith says you can do.

"WE MUST HAVE SOMETHING TO HEAR AND BELIEVE BEFORE WE CAN EXERCISE OUR FAITH.."

So, if we are to build our faith, we must spend time hearing and meditating on the Word of God. What are you believing God for right now? There is a Word from God for every situation in your life. If you are believing for the manifestation of physical healing, you need to pull healing scriptures.

1 Peter 2:24 states, "Who his own self bare our sins in his own body on the tree, that we being dead to sins should live unto righteousness: by whose stripes ye were healed." This is one of the scriptures that I meditated on

Sandra F. Holt

when I was believing God for my healing. I also pray this scripture over others as I remind them healing is a promise from God. All things are possible to them that believe. If you are believing for a financial blessing, Philippians 4:19 states, "But my God shall supply all your need according to his riches in glory by Christ Jesus." Whatever we are standing in the need of, God has given us His Word. Matthew 7 tells us God gives to those who ask.

2 Timothy 2:15 states, "Study to show thyself approved unto God, a workman that needeth not to be ashamed, rightly dividing the word of truth." Studying God's Word reveals His promises that are available to us. Not taking the time to find out what those promises are, is like having gifts available to you but never unwrapping the packages. I encourage you to open up God's Word which is full of His precious promises. Our faith continues to increase as we are open to the manifold promises of God.

"NOT TAKING THE TIME TO FIND OUT WHAT [GOD'S PROMISES] ARE IS LIKE HAVING GIFTS ...BUT NEVER UNWRAPPING THE PACKAGES."

The Bible states that the Word of God is like a seed sown in our hearts. Mark 4:20 states, "And these are they which are sown on good ground: such as hear the word, and receive it and bring forth fruit, some thirtyfold, some sixty, and some an hundred." Here we see that faith is when we hear God's Word and receive it.

What makes a farmer plant a crop in the ground is the belief that the ground will produce a harvest or crop.

44

The more seeds that are planted, the more crops will be produced. The planter is expecting a harvest from those seeds. The more we hear the Word of God, the more it gets into our hearts. The more of God's Word that gets in our hearts by faith, the more it will produce.

Are you ready for a harvest? Continue to allow the Word of God to come alive in your heart. Believe what God's Word says about you and expect results. When we have faith, the reward is promised and inevitable.

When we accepted God into our lives, what happened? Romans 10:8 states, "But what saith it? The word is nigh thee, even in thy mouth, and in thy heart: that is, the word of faith..." Verse 9 goes on to state, "if thou shalt confess with thy mouth the Lord Jesus, and shalt believe in thine heart that God hath raised him from the dead, thou shalt be saved." We accepted by faith that Jesus is the Son of God and that by our confession we would be saved.

We had to believe with our hearts and confess with our mouths. We had to believe that Jesus Christ did all the work on the cross. He died that we may live. Faith in God is what saved us and faith is what will keep us. The Word of God states that whosoever believe on Jesus shall not be ashamed and whosoever call on the name of the Lord shall be saved. Faith believes that.

I read a story about a young girl who was born without arms or legs due to a rare genetic condition which prevents limbs from developing properly in the womb.

Sandra F. Holt

Initially her life was filled with many disappointments and struggles. In addition to dealing with her disability, she was also bullied. She stated, "I'd go to sleep at night wishing I could just wake up and be like everyone else."

During this time, the girl's mom continued to believe that her daughter could live a normal life as she encouraged her daughter to be independent. During the child's middle teenage years, she unsuccessfully tried to commit suicide. I believe God had big plans for her. She did finally come to the resolve that her disability would no longer hold her back.

She started believing what her mother said about her. She made the decision that her physical condition or what other people said would not define her as she did have self-worth. She came to see that she was more in control of her happiness than she had initially realized. As an adult, she became a major speaker to businesses, prisons and schools. (Mel Johnson April 7, 2017).

This story should arouse our faith and cause us to realize that the only limits we have are the ones we place on ourselves. The young girl decided to see herself how God and her mom saw her, beautiful with so much to offer. Neither her disability nor her circumstances could hold her back now. She stepped out on her faith and began helping others live a life of ever-increasing faith.

Occasionally, I reminisce on how God saw me through the difficult time of being diagnosed with breast cancer. I knew that I had to allow God's Word to truly lead me. I could not depend on myself or even others. I had to let Him lead and guide me to keep me in perfect peace to know that everything was going to work out for me and thanks to the glory of God it did.

With my testimony, I am here today, not just a breast cancer survivor but I am a victory with faith. The enemy could not steal my faith. In fact, that situation grew my faith. From a natural perspective, I would not have chosen that route for my life but since it happened, I found out how to overcome and I truly came to see that I am more than a conqueror through Christ which strengthens me.

My faith taught me that. God taught me that. The Word states that if any man lack wisdom, let him ask of God. I asked and I received. The pain of that experience is long gone and only what is left is a memory of God's faithfulness and love for me during a very challenging time in my life.

Enemies of Faith :

FEAR, DOUBT AND UNBELIEF

As we focus on faith, we must be aware that there are hindrances or enemies to our faith that must be dealt with. Hindrances like fear, doubt, and unbelief run in a pack. The blessing is that faith will outperform them every time. Again, Hebrews 11:6 reminds us that it is a must that faith becomes part of our daily lives to even please God. As we walk by faith and not by sight, we must have our faith shoes on as God leads and guides us on a victorious path. When faith is exercised, what happens? The enemies of faith are unable to prevent us from accomplishing our desires.

Fear

In my book, *Goodbye Fear*, I talked about what fear is and what fear does. I discussed how fear is more than an emotion. Fear is an evil spirit from Satan that wants to keep us in bondage because fear is bondage. We should not allow fear to rule our lives as faith is our defense against Satan.

When we are tempted to live in fear, we must remember that we are children of God, and as His children God protects us and loves us. Fear may try to come but it can only take root in our hearts if we allow it. God is calling us to respond with our faith. When we use our faith in God by taking the shield of faith, the Bible states that we are able to quench every fiery darts of the enemy. We have a faith shield to handle fear.

Hebrews 10:23 states, "Let us hold fast the profession of our faith without wavering; (for he is faithful that promised;)." When I was a child, I always took pride in knowing that I was the daughter of Leonard and Anna McGhee. I never doubted their love and protection. If we can trust our natural parents, we

"FAITH IS READY TO HELP US OVERCOME AND BE VICTORIOUS."

should be encouraged and confident as God's children that God will deliver and save us from any attack of Satan. We should never doubt God's love and protection. Fear comes wanting us to think God will not protect and deliver us, but faith reminds us He will protect us. He is the same yesterday, today and forever more.

Doubt and Unbelief

Matthew 21 tells the story of Jesus approaching a fig tree that bare no figs. As a result, Jesus makes a profound statement that no fruit would ever grow on the fig tree again. The disciples witnessed the fig tree wither away. Jesus answered them, "...If you have faith, and **doubt not,** ye shall not only do this which is done to the fig tree, but also if ye shall say unto this mountain, Be thou removed, and be thou cast into the sea; it shall be done."

Here Jesus demonstrates what can be accomplished

Sandra F. Holt

absent of doubt. So, what is doubt? Doubt is "to call into question the truth of: to be uncertain. It is also to demonstrate a lack of confidence." Doubt is wondering if God is who He says He is and can He do what He says He can do. God wants us to have the full assurance and confidence that He is who He says He is and can do what He says He can do.

Doubt in its simplest form is intense questioning of the truth. We see this when Christ had risen from the dead and His disciple Thomas did not initially believe. After Jesus had risen from the dead, He appeared to the disciples, but Thomas was not with them. John 20:24-25 states,

> "But Thomas, one of the twelve, called Didymus, was not with them when Jesus came. The other disciples therefore said unto him, We have seen the LORD. But he said unto them, Except I shall see in his hands the print of the nails, and put my finger into the print of the nails, and thrust my hand into his side, I will not believe."

Thomas only believed what he could physically see. He questioned whether Jesus had risen from the dead based on his own reasoning. Based on that, he questioned the truth. When Jesus appeared again eight days later, "Jesus saith unto him, "Thomas, because thou hast seen me, thou hast believed: blessed are they that have not seen, and yet have believed." (John 20:29).

We are blessed when we believe what God says. A blessing is "the act or words of one that blesses." God is the blesser which causes the favor and blessings of God to be on our lives. Those of us who believe without seeing are blessed. Why? Because faith in God is a spiritual life that consists of a faith life that ultimately leads to a blessed life.

There may be many doubting Thomas's out there who at some point in their lives find themselves struggling to have faith. In fact, if I am to be truly transparent there have been many times in my life that I have struggled to believe. If others are honest, they will say the same; however, God never intended for faith to be a "hard pull." Think about your family member or even a dear friend that you know truly loves you. If you need something and you go to them, do you doubt whether they will help you? No.

"GOD NEVER INTENDED FAITH TO BE A HARD PULL."

You would not doubt them but often times we find ourselves doubting God. I heard a minister share a story about the late Charles Capps who noted every time he received an expense in the mail larger than what he could pay, he would say, "God, you got mail." This simple statement is a reminder that God ensures we have everything we need.

What if we make that simple statement every time we encounter a challenge, an obstacle that appears impossible? What if we give it to God instead of doubting

God? That's what faith does. That's what faith says, "God, you got mail."

We must continuously condition our minds to focus on the things of God and what God says about our situation. In my book *Goodbye Fear*, I talked about the mind and the powerful role the mind plays in our lives. I talked about Satan's ultimate job is to try to get us to doubt what God says about us or what God wants for us. God is calling us to exercise our faith and disregard every thought and lie from Satan by moving forward in the direction God desires us to go.

James 1:6 tells us that whatever we need we must ask in faith, not doubting. In fact, the Bible states he who doubts is "like a wave of the sea that is driven and tossed by the wind." Meaning you are unsettled, uncertain, not knowing what will happen. God's Word lets us know that a person who is unstable will not receive anything from God. There is a story in 2 Kings 7:1-2 that demonstrates doubt and unbelief:

> "Then Elisha said, Hear ye the word of the Lord, To-morrow about this time shall a measure of fine flour be sold for a shekel, and two measures of barley for a shekel, in the gate of Samaria. Then, a lord on whose hand the king leaned answered the man of God, and said, Behold, if the Lord would make windows in heaven, might this thing be? And he said, Behold, thou shall see it with thine eyes, but shalt not eat thereof."

God wants us to agree with what He says. In this passage the prophet was letting the people know in one day God was going to turn their situation around in a blessed way, although there had been a great famine in the land.

What happened? One of the king's soldiers looking literally with his physical eyes said that it was impossible to go from starving to flourishing in one day. As a result, the prophet of God responded to him by saying that he would witness this miracle, but he would not enjoy the miracle because of his unbelief.

That's exactly what happened. He witnessed it but he did not get to enjoy the miracle because he died before he was able to possess it. This story is a reminder of the importance of taking God at His Word and shun walking in doubt and unbelief.

If you are struggling with doubt and unbelief, I encourage you to list your struggles and present them before God to help you and strengthen you.

Lord, I am struggling in these areas:

1.

2.

3.

Sandra F. Holt

Faith Seal

When God says it is so. It is so. God wants us to seal
our hearts with faith regarding events beyond our control. Seal is defined "as a device or substance that joins
two things together to prevent them from coming apart."
We must have God's word in our hearts to keep us from
falling apart when trials come.

Once while remodeling our kitchen to replace the
tile with granite, the contractor informed me that once
the process was finished, he would
seal the granite. This is a good anal-
ogy as we think about what Jesus did
for us when He gave his life for us.
On the cross, He said, "It is finished."

> "WHEN WE BELIEVE GOD'S
> WORD AND TRUST GOD, WE
> FAITH-SEAL OUR LIVES."

Once Jesus sacrificed His life, He made a way for us
to be reconciled to Father God and that sealed it. He put
everything back in motion for us to live a blessed and
fulfilled life. When we believe God's Word and trust
God, we faith-seal our lives. We see then that fear, doubt
and unbelief are no match for our faith seal.

Again, as we welcome faith, the hindrances to our
faith cannot stay in our lives. No! We must leave them
behind. We must leave the pack of those enemies to our
faith, enemies to our blessings and enemies to our soul.
This reminds me of a story I read:

"A barber was walking through the city slums
with a minister, who said, 'This is why I can't

54

believe in a God of love. If He is as kind as they say, why does He permit all this poverty, disease...?' The minister remained silent until they met a man filthy and unkempt. His hair was hanging down his neck and his face unshaven.

The minister then replied, 'You can't be a very good barber or you wouldn't permit a man like that to continue living in this neighborhood without a haircut and a shave.'

The barber answered, 'Why blame me for that man's condition? I can't help it if he's like that. He has never given me a chance! If he would only come to my shop, I could fix him up and make him look like a gentleman!'

The minister gave the barber a penetrating look and said, 'Then don't blame God'.

I realize that some people are homeless for various reasons, including no fault of their own, but why do I share this story? Because often times people are looking for reasons not to believe and trust God. In this story, the barber was snared by his own words. He had a reason for why he did not help the unkempt man as the man had not come to him for help. When people do not accept or receive God by faith, it is not because God does not want

Sandra F. Holt

to help them. God says, "Whosoever will let him come."

As a reader you may ask, "But what about me? I have faith but I have not received help." Hebrews 4:16 states, "Let us therefore come boldly unto the throne of grace, that we may obtain mercy, and find grace to help in time of need." This scripture assures us that God will always help and deliver us and we should never doubt that God is not there for us. If you are doubtful ask God to help you to recognize His help and always be grateful for God's faithfulness.

> "UNBELIEF... IS KNOWING THE TRUTH BUT REFUSING TO BELIEVE IT."

Unbelief in simplest terms is knowing the truth but refusing to believe it and thus failing to act on the truth. I believe that unbelief is a choice. A choice not to believe. Unbelief keeps us from acting on God's Word and as a result, keeps us from receiving God's best for us.

Mark 9 tells the story of a father who wanted healing for his son. Jesus told the man that all things are possible if you believe. You see again how our faith is essential to get our miracle.

Jesus asked, "Do you believe that I can do it." The man replied with tears, "Lord, I believe; help thou mine unbelief." Here the man acknowledged that if there is any unbelief in him, he needed Jesus' help. Jesus showed compassion and healed the man's son.

This man's unbelief was not deliberate as he asked Jesus to help regarding any unbelief found in him. God does not want us to display deliberate unbelief because it does not please God. Hebrews 11:6 states in part, "...for he that cometh to God must believe that he is, and that he is a rewarder of them that diligently seek him."

Unbelief keeps the promises of God from being manifested in our lives. Mark 6 tells us that Jesus could not do mighty works in his own country because of their unbelief. This shows us that manifestation of God's power has a lot to do with our own faith.

Matthew 13:58 (NIV) also states, "And he did not do many miracles there because of their lack of faith." What was happening here? Jesus was trying to minister to his own hometown and perform miracles, but He could not because of their lack of faith. Notice here that the scripture does not say because of Jesus' lack of faith and neither does it say that Jesus did not have the power to perform miracles. No, it says for their lack of faith. This shows us that we each play an important part in what happens in our lives, in what is accomplished and the vital role that faith plays.

Hebrews 3 admonishes us to hear God's voice and harden not our hearts. Verse 12 (AMP) states, "Take care, brothers and sisters, that there not be in any one of you a wicked, unbelieving heart [which refuses to trust and rely on the Lord, a heart] that turns away from the living God."

Look at this. God does not want us to have an unbe-lieving heart which is a heart that refuses to trust and rely on God. Our hearts should be filled with the assurance of God's promises from His life-giving Word. We must purpose in our hearts to live a life of faith.

In fact, the Word of God states, "God's Word is the only truth and faith stands with the Word of God. There is a scripture that states "Had it not been for the Lord on my side, I would have fainted long ago." Knowing God is on our side regarding our hope, joy and peace should make all the difference in our lives.

We are on a journey with God being our guiding light. He is our hope and strength, and He is a rewarder of those that put their trust in Him. I have committed my life to trust God, even during times of uncertainty. I believe Him when He said that He will never leave me or forsake me even to the ends of the world. Faith must be our guiding light of trusting what God says and assist us in dealing with the enemies of our faith.

Other Enemies to our Faith

Spirit of Slothfulness

Did you know the spirit of slothfulness is an enemy to our faith? Why? Because faith is action. Many times when we are lazy, we are not honoring the gifts and talents God has given us.

God expects us to use our gifts and talents for His Glory. In fact, the Bible tells us that faith without works is dead. Faith transforms our lives when we act on God's Word.

Hello Faith

In Matthew Chapter 25, Jesus talks about the story where three individuals were provided talents to do incredible things. One was given five talents; another one was given two talents and a different individual was given one talent. The ones that were given five and two talents doubled their talents. Why? Because they did something with them. But what about the one who had only one talent?

He buried it. He didn't do anything with it. Know this, God does not expect us to compare ourselves to others. We each have a different set of fingerprints that makes us uniquely different from anyone else. In other words, God did not expect the person with one talent to say, "I have nothing to offer, I am not that person with five talents." No! but He does expect us to uniquely utilize our gifts and talents.

The man with one talent buried it. The Bible states that he didn't even collect interest on it; so, in essence, it was worth less than when he received it, especially if we factor in inflation. He allowed His talent to be devalued because he devalued its worth. Let me ask you a couple of questions?

Have you buried your talents or gifts God has given you? What do you do with something that is dead? The natural response maybe "to bury it" but my husband often says, "resurrect it." If you have buried your gifts or talents, I encourage you to resurrect them. Bring them back to life and start using your talents today! By Faith!

Sandra F. Holt

What About Unforgiveness?

When we are believing God to bless our lives, it is also important to know that we must also not allow unforgiveness to take root in our hearts. Unforgiveness is a hindrance to our faith. If you are to truly live a good and blessed life designed by God, you must purpose in your heart every day to walk in forgiveness and refuse to allow offenses to cause you to keep resentment in your heart.

Many times, hurting people walk in unforgiveness. The Bible tells us to forgive one another. Jesus tells us to constantly forgive. When Jesus was asked if we should forgive each other "seven times", Jesus replied, we should forgive "seventy times seven," meaning as many times as necessary which is exactly what Jesus has demonstrated for each of us.

Ephesians 4:32 states, "And be ye kind one to another, tenderhearted, forgiving one another, even as God for Christ's sake hath forgiven you." I encourage you to not allow unforgiveness to stand in the way of your blessings.

I make a decision to walk in forgiveness everyday. I realize that opportunities to walk in offense will always come. Unforgiveness is a snare to your faith that must be dealt with. If you are battling with unforgiveness ask God to purify your heart. Purpose in your heart that unforgiveness will not be a hindrance to your faith or hinder you from receiving the blessings God has for you.

In summary, hindrances or enemies to our faith can only accomplish what we allow them to. When we allow the hindrances to our faith to take root in our lives, they keep us from receiving our blessings and our miracles. Faith triumphs over these hindrances if exercised. I know for many years I exercised fear over faith.

I once allowed doubt and unbelief to manifest in my life. As a result, I opened the door to worry and anxiety. I worried as if that was going to change the situation. Maybe we unconsciously think worrying is accomplishing something when it is only causing more heartache. If we must do something, let's do it on our knees praying and trusting God.

> "HINDRANCES OR ENEMIES TO OUR FAITH CAN ONLY ACCOMPLISH WHAT WE ALLOW THEM TO."

Use your deductive reasoning. If we exercise our faith, something good will happen. Something good will manifest because we have put God's Word in action. Let's remove the hindrances. Let's remove them today!

Sandra F. Holt

Take a moment and Identify any Hindrances to your Faith.

Hindrances to my Faith Worksheet

_____

_____

_____

_____

_____

_____

_____

_____

_____

_____

_____

_____

_____

_____

_____

_____

_____

_____

Dare to Dream

I believe God is calling us to dream and live our best lives and yes, we accomplish this through faith. As we look at the life of Joseph in the Bible, we see how God blessed him to have dreams and interpretation of dreams. Joseph would often times share his dreams with his family and it finally got to the point that his brothers would say, "There goes that dreamer." They were making a mockery of his dreams, but the more he dreamed, I believe the more he got comfortable with the dreams that were coming from within him and the more he could see those dreams fulfilled.

"DREAMING IGNITES FAITH."

When we trust God, then we become dreamers and get comfortable with the calling on our lives. We should all have dreams inside of us to make our lives better, to make our family lives better and ultimately to make the world better. Dreaming, in essence, ignites our faith; it grows our faith. We see things from a different perspective.

Tests may come in our lives to cause us to keep the faith and hold on to those big dreams from God. Joseph ultimately gained the favor of the pharaoh (a high status) of Egypt, and the wealth of Egypt. It did not stop there though. He became the one that prepared Egypt for a time of famine. Due to the famine, Joseph's brothers left

Sandra F. Holt

their homeland and came to Egypt for food.

This allowed Joseph to play a major role in ensuring his family had enough food in the time of shortage. I encourage you to read this story in Genesis. In this story, Joseph demonstrated forgiveness and mercy to his brothers who had once betrayed him. They may not have believed in his dreams, but their unbelief could not stop the fulfillment of the dreams that God placed inside of Joseph.

As I was meditating and letting God know things that I was desiring from Him, I felt

"DON'T LET SITUATIONS OR PEOPLE ABORT YOUR DREAM."

God speaking to me saying, "Don't let situations or even people abort your dreams." Abort means to terminate or give up on seeing the dreams fulfilled. Joseph's brothers did not believe in his dreams, but he kept dreaming. Sometimes we can even be in our own way to see our dreams fulfilled or occasionally allow others around us who are not dreamers to discourage us.

Maybe you have shared your dreams with others only to see them go into abort mode or shared your dreams with people who are only looking at your current state. That's how Joseph's brothers initially saw him, but when they came to see "that dreamer" whom they had mocked was the food supply for them, they changed their opinion. That's what happens when you dream big and hold unto what God has placed inside of you. It changes others' opinions, even those who mocked you.

I have come to see in my personal life that everyone who says they are supporting you may not, but that should not deter you from dreaming. Dreams are a blessing from God and when we keep dreaming and believing God, as Joseph accomplished amazing and wonderful things, so shall we. We, too, will say like Joseph, "I am in the place of God." Being in the place of God reminds us that this is where God has always meant for us to be as we see the reality of our dreams displayed.

I read a powerful story about a young boy who received an "F" on his English paper because he dared to dream. He was the son of a horse trainer. They would go to many ranches training horses. As a result, his schoolwork was not up to part. During his senior year, he was asked to write a paper about what he wanted to be and do when he grew up. He wrote a seven-page paper describing his goal of someday owning a horse ranch.

He was very specific as he drew a floor plan for a 4,000-square-foot house that would sit on a 200-acre dream ranch. He turned the paper into his teacher but two days later he received the paper back. On the front of the paper was a red "F" with a note that read, "See me after class."

He went to see the teacher after class and asked, "Why did I receive an F?" The teacher said "This is an unrealistic dream for a young boy like you." The teacher noted that if he went back and rewrote his paper with a more realistic dream, she would reconsider his grade.

Sandra F. Holt

He went home and thought about it. After about a week, the boy returned the paper, making no changes to it at all. He stated to the teacher, "You can keep your "F" and I'll keep my dream." (Ashland Times Gazette, March 27, 2017).

I am inspired by this story and the determination of the young boy as he refused to allow the teacher to abort his dream. As I continued to read the story, it revealed that he did receive all that he dreamed about. During an interview regarding his life he noted, "I still have that school paper framed over the fireplace." Although the teacher tried to abort his dream, that became his motivation.

I would like to believe that the "F" in the little boy's eyes changed from "Fail" to "Faith." The message in this story is a reminder that there are a lot of dream stealers, but our faith triumphs over them. We must constantly remember that no one can destroy our dreams unless we permit them. We need to say to Satan, "You keep your lies and deceptions. I am going to keep my dreams. I will keep my Faith!"

One of the characteristics of a dreamer is he or she never gives up. That's faith in action. Even writing this book was a dream, and my faith made it happen. I had to listen to the voice of God and write this book, although many times dismissing my own thoughts that it was an impossible task to accomplish with everything else, I had to do. Faith caused me to discipline myself to sit at my computer and just write, believing I would produce a book that will bless people. When distractions came, I kept writing. I was seeing the dream fulfilled, I was seeing the book already written.

Genesis 28:12–13 (in part) states, "And he dreamed, and behold a ladder set up on the earth, and the top of it reached to heaven: and behold the angels of God ascending and descending on it. And behold, the Lord stood above it..."

This scripture is referring to Jacob's dream. In Jacob's dream, God allowed him to see angels going up and coming down from heaven as God stood at the top of the stairway. The scripture goes on to reveal the plans and the promises that God had for Jacob's life. Just like

"DREAM AS IF THERE ARE NO LIMITS, NO HINDRANCES. DREAM, DREAM, DREAM."

God had great plans for Jacob, in the simplest form, this is a reminder that God wants the best for us and those dreams that are inside of us are not our own initial ideas but they have been placed inside of us by God. If He put the dreams inside of us, we can be assured that they will come to pass.

Give yourself permission to dream. I don't care how impossible it may seem. Dream as if there are no limits, no hindrances. Dream, dream, dream, and as you are dreaming, use your faith in God's Word to make it happen. He wants us to dream without limits.

Dream BIG! God wants us to use our imaginations

Sandra F. Holt

because He made our imaginations. The truth is, we can dream as big as our imagination, and we can accomplish as little as we limit our imagination. Ultimately, we will come to see, big dreams prove we have a big God. What are you believing God for?

Maybe your dreams are material: pay that house off, get out of debt, or maybe travel around the world. Do you know all of those examples are possible? When faith becomes your partner, it is achievable because I believe faith connects us to our dreams and dreams connect us to our faith as everything is ultimately connected to our Big God.

What are you dreaming about?

1.

_____

_____

_____

2.

_____

_____

_____

3.

_____

_____

_____

It's Not Too Late

If you are at a point in your life wherein you are no longer dreaming, I feel led to tell you that it is not too late to go for your heart's desires. Wake up those dreams that have laid dormant in your life. I never imagined being a writer. I have always been opened to God using me but I never imagined writing.

In my book *Goodbye Fear* I talked about how you have unlimited potential. It's time to tap into that unlimited potential inside of you. Have faith that God has great plans for you. Don't be afraid.

> "ENJOY THE FAITH RIDE BECAUSE GOD IS THE DRIVER."

I hear Him saying that just like I was with Moses, Joshua... I am with you. Faith is NOW! It is time to move now. This is a new chapter in your life. It is full of excitement and potential Now! It is a new chapter in mine.

Enjoy the faith ride because God is the driver, and He will never steer us wrong. Faith says I can do all things. Faith says for with God nothing is impossible. Faith says it is yours for the asking, receiving and believing.

I heard a lady talk about when she felt her life was in a rut as she would keep the same routine every day. After work, she would come home and watch other people live their dreams. Maybe some of you feel like your life is in a rut, almost saying, "I know, it is more to life than this."

As for me, I had perfected my cheerleader routine for others but I found myself being my worse cheerleader; but not anymore. I came to see that it is important to support other's dreams and cheer for them, but it is as equally important to focus on my dreams as well.

When God started speaking to me about writing a book and helping others take better care of their bodies by eating healthier, it was as if a light bulb came on. I realized it was time to recharge my life (or faith-charge my life.) I decided that I was no longer going to watch the ship go by and watch others fulfill their dreams. I was going to use my faith to fulfill my own dreams.

I decided, by faith, that I was going to put what God has placed in my heart on the pages of a book to bless others. I also decided I would put in the hours of research to show others the benefits of eating healthier. I was ready to use my gifts. I was igniting my faith.

I recall when I was in college, I met a young lady at the time that had no dreams, no aspirations. It was very sad now that I think back on our conversation. Although she was thankful for the basic necessities of life, she was not motivated and had no drive to make her life even better.

Don't get me wrong. We should all be thankful for the basic necessities of life, but I believe she was just existing and not living. I remember her making statements like, "I guess I should be thankful I have a bed, a job..."

As she talked, she seemed to get sadder and sadder.

At times, I did not know what to say to her, so I just listened. Even to this day, I see the sadness in her eyes. During our conversation, although we were both young, I saw myself on a different path than she was as I focused on the opportunities that awaited me.

Maybe it was something that transpired in her life to make her feel like she had to settle with where she was and in essence caused her to struggle with finding fulfillment in her life. I don't know, but it was obvious to me that she was not dreaming, and her vision of life created a bleak picture. She seemed in a rut as she settled with where she was.

Please know, God does not want us to settle. He tells us in Isaiah 1:19: "If you are willing and obedient, ye shall eat the good of the land." Some translations say, "The best of the land." God desires the best for me, but I must also desire it for myself. God does not want us to love things. He wants us to love Him and others and use things to bless others. He wants us to embrace life with excitement and passion. I can only hope that life finally did bring her more fulfillment.

Are you in a rut? I encourage you to come out of that rut. There is so much more that God wants you to do. There is so much more to you.

See, when we do our part, we should expect God to do His. When my daughters were teenagers, I would tell them, "I will be back and if I come back and the house is clean, we will go shopping." When I arrived home, guess what? The house was clean. Although my youngest daughter moved a little slower, she got there. That's what God wants us to do. Get there!

We must yield our lives to what God Words says as we take His promises to live a fulfilled life. That's why I love seeing younger people become entrepreneurs. They can inspire all ages to start dreaming again, start believing again, start hoping again and remove all limits.

That's what my daughters and son-in-law did for me. In fact, I must admit God used them to cause me to get out there and utilize my gifts. Thank you, Brittany, Jeremy and Brandi!

Whatever you are believing God for, I encourage you to hold on to it. It will manifest. Faith says that what I desire is mine for the asking. Faith stands on the Word of God. I remember a teacher literally had me in fear about my writing. Now I am writing books and depositions. That is faith.

Keep striving; keep reaching for the stars. Keep believing God. Keep pressing toward your goal. I encourage you to dream your best life.

What does that mean? Create in your mind how you want to see yourself, your life, and be open to God, using your faith to make it happen. It is achievable; it is possible; it is faith.

I often hear the saying "time is winding up" but I heard a minister say, "You were never meant to serve time, but time was meant to serve you." That is a profound statement. So often we think time "has run out." Many believe it is too late to see their dreams fulfilled. So many spend their life wishing they had taken another direction or believing it is too late to change course.

Faith doesn't focus on time but the Word of God. That's a benefit of faith. What if the woman with the issue of blood for 12 long years had focused on her situation believing she had little time? Would she have received her healing? Maybe not. The truth is she did not have any natural means left to get the healing she needed. She needed nothing less than a miracle. Having the faith that she could get better produced that miracle for her.

> **"FAITH DOESN'T FOCUS ON TIME BUT THE WORD OF GOD."**

She refused to be denied her miracle. I just want to encourage you to know that as long as breath is in your body, you can move towards fulfilling your dreams whether it is for your health, finances, concerns for a family member or friend; whatever it is, all things are possible to them that believe.

The Bible states write the vision. What does that mean? To keep your desires, dreams constantly before your eyes. Use your faith, seeing that what you are believing for is already done.

When I was in High school, I used to run track and I thoroughly enjoyed this sport. I remember everyone on the team had to provide their shoe sized in order for their

Sandra F. Holt

cleats to be ordered. I gave my size along with others. When the cleats came back, I saw that mine were too small. The coach asked me, "What are you going to do?"

I stated that I was going to wear my regular gym shoes on the field. Unfortunately, I came to see my regular gym shoes were not the best to run in a race. On competition day, I was ready to run the 100 meters. Guess what happened? When we were told to go, I slipped and fell down. Why? Because I had the wrong shoes on. Needless to say, I just had to leave the field. There was no way to catch up.

> "YOU ARE NEVER TO OLD TO CHASE A DREAM OR EVEN TRY AGAIN."

Maybe that's where you are. You feel as if you are unable to fulfill the dreams you once wanted to accomplish in life because you think it is too late. You are never too old to chase a dream or to even try again. It may not be exactly how you initially envisioned it or the way you initially wanted it to be, but you must know, it is achievable.

Maybe in life you did a lot of slipping and falling, and now you are looking at where you are. Maybe you have that book draft that you been holding on for 10 or 20 years. It is not too late to start writing. It's not too late to fulfill those dreams. I would like to encourage you that God is truly a restorer.

Joel 2:25 (CEV) states in part, "I, the LORD your God, will make up for the losses caused by those swarms and swarms of locusts..." Another translation states, "I will compensate you…" This is encouraging and a reminder that it is never too late even if you caused trouble to come in your life due to disobedience. If you repent, God can restore you back on the path He desires for you. Remember, He is the one that completes us.

I remember sitting on the bench feeling sad that I could not participate in any of the races. I felt I had let myself and the team down. I was feeling sorry for myself. Apparently, the coach had compassion on me because he looked at one of my teammates and said, "Give Sandra your cleats."

I can hear the coach even now saying those words, "Give Sandra your cleats." I was filled with joy and excitement. I had another opportunity to run in a race. Thank you Coach Robertson! That's what God does for us when we embrace faith.

That's what I am doing for you. I am giving you the cleats of encouragement to get back in the race. It was not too late for me in that race, and it is not too late for you now!

Abraham's Evolving Faith

As believers in Jesus Christ, we are the seed of Abraham. In fact, Galatians 3:29 states, "And if ye be Christ's, then are ye Abraham's seed, and heirs according to the promise." This tells us that since we belong to Christ, we are part of Abraham's family and just as Abraham believed by faith then we must believe by faith.

In Genesis 12, God tells Abram (before his name was changed to Abraham), "Get the out of thy country... And I will make of thee a great nation, and I will bless thee, and make thy name great; and thou shalt be a blessing..."

Look at the manifold promises of God to Abram. Two words that stand out to me: great and blessing. He provides Abram instructions and lets him know what will happen when he follows those instructions. Think about it; when God called Abram to leave His country, He promised to bless him, make his name great, and through him all the families of the earth would be blessed.

God's blessings are associated with happiness, peace, joy and prosperity in our lives. So, when we walk by faith, we are living God's promises over our lives. We are living in God's overflow for our lives because faith embraces those promises. Faith says they are ours.

As I read the story of Abram, I can only imagine that it may have been easy for Abram to leave his country, but I do wonder how difficult it was for him to leave his family. I don't really know what Abram was thinking as the Bible does not provide insight, however in Genesis 12:5, it tells us that Abram did take Lot, his brother's son with him. Some theologians debate as to whether Abram was totally obedient since he took Lot with him when God said leave your country and kindred; nonetheless, it appears God saw Abram's actions overall as an act of obedience.

Is it possible that Abram wanted to protect Lot? Did he want a better life for Lot? Again, I don't know. This part of the story is a little personal to me as I ended up moving from my hometown after graduating from college. After initially graduating from college, I was having difficulty finding a job because the company that I had been working with every summer decided not to pick up their summer hires.

My baby sister at the time had a small baby and in my finite wisdom, I thought I needed to take care of them, although she was married with a family. I also wanted to stay to help my dad with his Church ministry. While applying for various jobs, it appeared every door seemed to close in my face. I desperately wanted a job in my own home state in Mississippi.

I was denied one job after another. In fact, I was told in one job interview, I was competing with too much experience. As I look back after so many years, could it be God wanted me to leave my hometown and go on the journey He had planned for me? I ended up leaving my birthplace and moving to Tennessee. I was not ready to leave but I did. When I arrived in Tennessee, my loving aunt welcomed me into her home as one of her own children.

It seemed like things began to fall in place immediately and doors opened. Within a very short period of time, I started receiving job offers. Although I felt I needed to be in one place, God showed me where He wanted me to be.

"WHEN WE SEEK GOD AND TRUST HIM, HE WILL ALWAYS MAKE US TO LIE DOWN IN GREEN PASTURES..."

Wherever life takes us, we must know God wants the best for us and the story will always end in a blessed life. It was there that I met my husband (now of 35 years.) We must know that the plans God has for us always causes life situations to work out. I also did not have to worry about my baby sister and father's ministry. Everything worked out fine. I was able to assist my father in the ministry when I could and enjoyed spending time with my nephew.

Maybe you are at a crossroad in your life wondering what direction to go. When we seek God and trust Him, He will always make us to lie down in green pastures and lead us besides the still waters as stated in Psalm 23. Ask God what His plans are for your life. Ask Him to reveal His perfect plan for your life.

When He does, He expects you to follow them. Faith

in what God says must be the center of our focus. God knows what's best for us and He will never steer us wrong on this life's journey.

The word tells us that Abram departed as the Lord had spoken. What if we just obey what God tells us to do? If we do, we are assured blessings that overflow. Jeremiah 29:11, my baby sister's favorite scripture, states, "For I know the thoughts that I think toward you, saith the Lord, thoughts of peace, and not evil, to give you an expected end." We can take comfort in knowing God desires so much to bless us and His thoughts towards us are good and perfect even as He is perfect. We don't need to worry about the future when we know our lives are in God's hands.

God appeared to Abram again in Genesis 12 and God promised Abram that He would give him land, and Abram built an altar before the Lord recognizing God's lordship. God appeared again to Abram in Genesis 13:14 -16 and says,

"Lift up now thine eyes, and look from the place where thou art northward, and southward, and eastward, and westward: For all the land which thou seest, to thee will I give it, and to thy seed forever: And I will make thy seed as the dust of the earth: so that if a man can number the dust of the earth, then shall thy seed be numbered."

In verse 17 God says, "Arise, walk through the land

in the length of it and in breadth of it; for I will give it unto thee." As I meditate on Genesis, chapters 12 and 13, I see God continuously speaking to Abram and sharing His promises. I believe that the more God spoke, the more faith was being born in Abram. The more we read God's Word and take hold of the promises, the more faith is being born.

When we go through the trials of life and God brings us out as we put our trust in Him, there is a change taking place in us. The more our faith is being born. In Genesis 15:1 God appears to Abram in a vision saying, "Fear not Abram: I am thy shield and thy exceeding great reward." He tells Abram that He is Abram's protection. Once God appears this time, Abram says to God, "Lord God, what wilt thy give me, seeing I go childless...Behold, to me thou hast given no seed: and, lo, one born in my house is mine heir." From a natural standpoint the question makes since.

After all, Abram was aging and the only heir appeared to be his servant. But the word of the Lord that came to Abram in Genesis 15:4 states,"...This shall not be thine heir; but he that shall come forth out of thine own bowels shall be thine heir." God told Abram he would father a child with his own seed. Verse 5 states, "And he brought him forth abroad, and said, Look now toward heaven, and tell the stars, if thou be able to number them: and he said unto him, So shall thy seed be."

Genesis 15:6 states that Abram "believed in the

Lord, and He accounted it to him for righteousness." Look at this, God was repeating His promises to Abram over and over again. Abram was hearing and hearing the promises and the word says that he believed God. God continued to confirm His word to Abram as He kept placing His promises before Abram.

You see, God wants us to take His promises and hold onto them. We must keep them before our face, before our eyes. Every time Abram looked at his situation from a natural perspective, God showed Abram the outcome from a supernatural perspective.

Could it be that part of the challenge with believing is that we look for the answer in the natural when the answer is always supernatural because our God is supernatural. The idea that Abram was getting older from a natural perspective could not alter God's promises. The fact they you have not received your manifestation to what you are believing God for does not alter God's promises.

Genesis 16 continues to give us an account of what was going on in Sarai (Abram's wife) and Abram's mind. They still had no children, so Sarai allowed Abram to father a child by someone else. So many times, we look for ways to get what we want by trying to assist God. I know there have been times in my life I felt God was moving slower than I preferred as I wanted Him to move a little faster.

In my finite wisdom, I tried to assist God only to

find myself back at following God's ultimate plans for my life. To me, the saying, "He may not come when you want Him, but He is always on time" is a profound statement that is validated 100% by God's actions and faithfulness; however, I believe this statement is supernatural.

Abram had promises from God although there was no natural manifestation, so he abided by his wife's request and Sarai's maiden, Hagar, conceived a child named Ishmael. Abram was 86 years old when Ishmael was born. The Bible is silent as to whether God appeared to Abram after Ishmael was born until we get to Genesis 17, when Abram was 99 years old or 13 years later. God appeared to Abram and told Abram all that He would do in multiplying his seed and that he would be the father of many nations.

God also changed Abram's name to Abraham. In Hebrew, Abram means exalted father but Abraham means father of a multitude. The power in a name. God also changed Sarai's name to Sarah. Then God said I will bless you and give you a son from Sarah. Abraham responded with "shall a child be born to me at 100 and Sarah at 90?"

God then got specific saying Sarah shall bare a son and his name shall be Isaac. Abraham laughed. The Bible acknowledges that Abraham and Sarah were well stricken in age, but the Lord God said that Sarah would bear a child. In fact, when the word came that Sarah would conceive, she laughed. God came back and responded, "Is there anything too hard for the Lord?"

If you are facing insurmountable odds, this verse should encourage you and it has truly encouraged me. God was not moved by time. He was not moved by Abraham and Sarah's age. God is only moved by His Word and faith in God's Word works.

So, what happened? Genesis tells us that Sarah conceived and bore Abraham a son in their old age. Sarah said, "God hath made me to laugh, so that all that hear will laugh with me." Yes, faith makes us laugh because it reminds us that God can and will accomplish what He said He would do regardless of how impossible it looks. Faith always has the last word that makes us rejoice every time.

Abraham was 100 years old when Isaac was born. I looked up the number 100. It represents new beginnings, fresh starts, and infinite possibilities. It symbolizes unity. If only we can see that faith in God represents infinite possibilities when we unite our faith with what God's Word says. This story about Abraham is so insightful. Abram, who is now Abraham, started with promises from God that appeared to be impossible promises from a natural perspective.

God kept the promises before Abraham with His Words. That's faith in the highest form. It does not matter what the obstacles are in the natural, it focuses on the promises in the supernatural. These promises to Abraham appeared from a natural perspective to be unachievable

Sandra F. Holt

with each passing year.

Maybe you are in a situation and the years continue to pass by with no perceived manifestation. I encourage you to not focus on what your eyes see in the natural but look to the promises of God in the spiritual. God's promises says that all things are possible to them that believe. If you can believe it, it is possible. If you can see it in the spiritual, it is possible. If you put God's Word on it, it is possible.

We serve an all knowing, all powerful and all present God. Nothing can stop God's plans. He wants us to exercise our faith. He wants us to know beyond a shadow of doubt that it is already done. With the powerful God we serve, nothing can stop His Word from manifesting. We are God's masterpiece, and He has the Master Plan for our lives. In fact, the Bible states that before we were formed in our mother's womb God knew us.

> "FAITH IN ACTION PUTS GODS WORD ON THE LINE."

Successful people are willing to put everything on the line to succeed. Faith in action puts God's Word on the line. Hebrews 6 tells us that when God made promises to Abraham, He swore by himself. There was no one greater that He could swear by saying to Abraham, "Surely blessing I will bless thee, and multiplying I will multiply thee." This was the ultimate confirmation because it was spoken by God. After Abraham patiently endured, he received the promise.

84

As I continue to read and to meditate on the story of Abraham, my faith continues to be supercharged. I thank God for revelation. He truly is our exceeding and great reward. He is our promise keeper. He is our all in all.

I know who I am, and I know He is able to keep you and me during any test or trial in our lives. The Bible tells us that the shield of faith is armour. Could it be when we take the shield of faith to quench the fiery darts of the enemy, God is going on the front lines for us; therefore the enemy has to face God because we are using our faith in God's Word that defeats Satan every time.

"GOD IS GOING ON THE FRONT LINES FOR US."

As God continued to remind Abraham of God's promises, it kept getting deeper into his spirit. As we read God's word and meditate on God's word, we cause those impossible situations to look possible. What's impossible in your life right now? Do you have a promise from God? Do you have the faith?

If you do, you can just enter into the land of possibilities. That is what happened to Abraham. Possibly with every passing year where he saw no evidence, he had to cast down those thoughts that his dreams had not been fulfilled. But he kept going because God kept speaking. When he was obedient enough to leave his home and his familiar place, his obedience exemplified the faith that God was about to perfect with blessings that began to overflow in his life.

As a result, Isaac was born. Maybe you are facing overwhelming odds, know that your Isaac will be born. Isaac is symbolic of the miracle that you need that can only come from God. It will come forth because God said it. Joshua 1:8 states we should meditate on God's Word and to do all that is written, and this will make our way prosper. Meditating on God's word is an action that will assist in birthing that Isaac every time.

Genesis 18 also displays the power of God's Words. Sodom and Gomorrah's sins had come before the eyes of God, but the angel of God says something profound prior to God destroying the city due to their sins. God says in vs. 17-18, "Shall I hide from Abraham that thing which I shall do; Seeing that Abraham shall surely become a great and mighty nation, and all the nations of the earth shall be blessed in him?"

This is powerful. This shows us that God's Words are irreversible. He proclaimed Abraham's greatness. The Bible states that the gifts and callings are irreversible. But guess what, Satan's lies and words are reversible if we exercise our faith.

Genesis 18:19 "For I know him, that he will command his children and his household after him, and they shall keep the way of the Lord, to do justice and judgment; that the Lord may bring upon Abraham that which he hath spoken of him."

God speaks the promises over Abraham's life, but He also says that He knows Abraham, and he will command his children to follow after God. What does God know about you? No doubt, Abraham was destined to live faith. If Abraham was destined to live faith, then as the seeds of Abraham, we are also.

My daughter shared with me how my grandson blessed her one day with his faith. He wanted to be selected to be in a group at his school. He shared with his mom that he expected to be selected. In my daughter's mind, she wanted to protect her son from disappointment, so she stated, "JK, it's okay if you are not chosen." After she made that statement to him, he said to his mom, "Mom, don't be negative. Each day I will go to school expecting to be selected. If I am not selected that day, I will go to school the next day, expecting to be selected. I will not give up."

Wow! Look at faith through the eyes of a child. This firm faith from a five-year-old truly blessed me. What if our faith was like that? What if we raised our level of expectation like that? What if we had the attitude that not receiving what we wanted was not an option?

This is a lesson for all ages. In fact, If you are believing God for some great things to manifest in your life, you may want to bring a child in your prayer circle to believe with you. I sure will be including my little grandson. Amen.

After Abraham finally received a son, he faced the ultimate test as recorded in Genesis 22. God told Abraham to offer his only son to God as a sacrifice. Abraham

Sandra F. Holt

rose up early in the morning and he and Isaac went to the place God told him. When Isaac saw the wood burning for the sacrifice, he asked where was the sacrifice; Abraham responded, "God will provide a sacrifice."

Abraham built an altar and was about to sacrifice Isaac when an angel of the Lord told him not to harm the child. Abraham showed by his actions that he feared God to the point of not even withholding his only son. We get a glimpse of Abraham's faith when Isaac asked Abraham 'where was the lamb for the burnt offering' and Abraham responded, "God will provide himself a lamb for the burnt offering." He did not say to Isaac, "You are it."

Maybe Abraham thought about his son being born to him where blessings would flow through or he thought about the promises God had made as he prepared to offer Isaac as a sacrifice. With those thoughts, I believe Abraham's faith was evolving. Faith had become a part of Him. He and faith were becoming inseparable.

The author of Hebrews elaborates on Abraham's faith. Hebrews 11:17-19 states, "By faith Abraham, when he was tried, offered up Isaac and he that received the promises offered up his only begotten son", vs. 18 "Of whom it was said, That in Isaac shall thy seed be called": vs. 19, "Accounting that God was able to raise him up, even from the dead; from whence also he received him in a figure."

Here, I believe we see Abraham's faith had evolved into great faith. God had already told Abraham that Isaac would be the seed of the promise so Abraham was convinced that God could or would raise Isaac from the dead. Are you encouraged by this? Our God is all-powerful? Where is your faith? Is it little faith, medium faith or great faith?

The test of offering up a son finally conceived by Abraham and Sarah in their old age was the ultimate test to build Abraham's faith to evolve into great faith. We may not like tests from a natural perspective, but we need to get the revelation that each test is building our spiritual muscles and moving us to greater faith.

"WE MAY NOT LIKE TESTS...BUT WE NEED TO GET THE REVELATION THAT EACH TEST IS BUILDING OUR SPIRITUAL MUSCLES."

I love my two grandchildren singing a song they learned at school: *My God is so Big*: Some of the lyrics according to my grandson says: "My God is so big; My God is so mighty; There is nothing my God cannot do for you. The mountains are His; The valleys are His; The trees are His handiwork too."

This is a powerful song. I believe Abraham came to see that in the ultimate test that His God is so big and there is nothing that His God cannot do (for you!). Before Abraham could offer Isaac up as a sacrifice, the angel of the Lord called Abraham and said to not sacrifice the child and stated, "for now I know that thou fearest God, seeing thou hast not withheld thy son, thine only son from me." Abraham lifted his eyes and looked and saw a ram caught in a thicket and Abraham took the ram and offered to God instead of his son.

This is a reminder that God never expects anything from us that He does not expect of Himself. Ultimately, God gave His Son, Jesus, that we might be set free from the bondage of sin and death. In essence, Jesus was the ultimate sacrifice. After this incident, Abraham called the place Jehovah-Jireh (meaning the Lord will provide). Because of Abraham's willingness to be obedient, He was reminded in Genesis 22:18, "And in thy seed shall all the nations of the earth be blessed; because thou hast obeyed my voice."

God swore by Himself telling Abraham that he would multiply Abraham's seed as the stars in heaven. What awesome news. Every believer is a seed of Abraham's multiplied blessings and if Abraham was blessed then we are blessed!

You see how God appeared personally to Abraham multiple times proclaiming His promises to Abraham and each time developing faith in his life? It is these promises of God, these covenants from God, that Abraham's faith is founded upon. Abraham was a man of faith because he knew and believed God as he allowed his faith to grow and trust God against overwhelming odds. Because of his great faith, he opened up heaven's blessings to his descendants which include every believer who exercises his or her faith in God's Word.

I am so blessed by reading the story of Abraham

and my prayer is that you are too as I walk you through various accounts of Abraham's faith in this book. Abraham had no physical evidence, but he was motivated; he was encouraged by God's promises. This should ignite our hope. This should ignite our faith.

God wants us to believe His Word, and He knows how to stir our faith. You may not see the natural evidence of that big house. You may not feel your body is healed. You may not see that promotion in the natural, but faith does see it. Faith

"FAITH WILL ALWAYS SEE THROUGH THE EYES OF OUR BORN-AGAIN SPIRIT."

will always distinguish us from what our physical eyes see. Faith will always distinguish us from hopelessness and despair. Faith will always see through the eyes of your born-again spirit.

As the Spirit of God allowed me to meditate on the process that Abraham went through and how his faith was growing during very challenging times in his life, it is a constant reminder that his faith was ever evolving. His faith was ever growing. Are you inspired to exercise your faith to receive the promises of God? I know I am.

Abraham's life encourages me to know that regardless of the challenges and circumstances we face, they cannot stop the promises and plans God has for us as we evolve as conquerors in every area of our lives. Thank God for allowing us to see Abraham's faith evolving.

My Faith: Ever Evolving

I enjoyed reading parts of Michelle Obama's book, *Becoming*. She talks about stages in her life as she continued to become. I must admit that I see myself like that with faith. I may not have produced my faith yet in some of the ways of several of the great men and women known in the Bible, but ultimately, I am coming to see in my own faith walk that my faith is becoming, ever evolving, ever increasing even through my struggles, as I put my ultimate trust in God. As I exercise my faith, I see God growing me up so that I continue to evolve into the person He predestined me to be.

God's Word brings light and illumination into our spirit, into our situation. It is God's Word and faith in God's Word that cause me to realize that I have to become inseparable with faith. 1 Corinthians 2:9 states "But as it is written, Eye hath not seen, nor ear heard, neither have entered into the heart of man, the things which God hath prepared for them that love him." This scripture reminds me that God has so much in store for me as my faith continues to evolve because faith opens Heaven's warehouse that constantly puts me in amazement.

I see the necessity to decide every day that I will walk by faith. I repeat. I must decide every day to walk by faith. Why do I make that decision? Because it causes me to surrender to the Word of God by reading it, and reading it, until faith takes root in my heart. I know I must do what God said to develop my faith and as I do, it will grow. It is growing.

Acts 17:28 states in part, "For in him we live, and move, and have our being..." God wants us to come to that revelation. How do we come to that revelation? By spending time with Him, meditating on His Word. Praising Him and letting Him know how much we love Him.

God says to seek Him and we shall find Him when we search for Him with all our hearts. Are you seeking Him? Are you chasing Him? If you are, He is right there.

"WE ARE WATCHING OURSELVES BEING CREATED INTO WHO GOD HAS ALREADY PERFECTED US TO BE."

We must make a point to spend quality time with Him. I have found times in my life that I receive a gentle nudge from the Holy Spirit to get up and spend time with Him. This simple nudge reminds me that I am becoming. When I deny myself and do what God instructs me to do, I am becoming. When I make a conscientious effort to live the life God desires for me, I am becoming.

When I decide to walk in the love and the peace of God, I am becoming. When I decide to walk in forgiveness, I am becoming. When I make the decision to welcome faith, I am becoming.

As I have been led by the Spirit of God to write this book, I see that there are areas of my life where I have

Sandra F. Holt

walked in greater faith, but there are areas God is still working on. I see, I must give myself permission to grow in faith. The Word says to grow in the Lord and the knowledge of Him. The more you know, the more you grow. The scripture states, "Man shall not live by bread alone but by every word that proceeded out of the mouth of God." (Deut. 8:3; Matt. 4:4)

I often look at life as a large puzzle with many pieces. Each day, we put those pieces together. Some days it appears harder to put the pieces together, but we must keep working on the puzzle because that puzzle is the master picture that has already been created. In essence, we are watching ourselves being created into who God has already perfected us to be.

> "OUR LIVES ARE LIKE...PUZZLES. AS WE GET OLDER AND BECOME MORE MATURE, THE PIECES OF OUR PUZZLES BECOME MORE COMPLEX."

My grandchildren have had various puzzles. When they were younger, their puzzles were comprised of bigger pieces. However, as they get older, the puzzle pieces get smaller with more complexity. Our lives are like those puzzles. As we get older and become more mature, the pieces of our puzzle become more complex, which is why it is important for our faith to continue to evolve. As the pieces get smaller, it will take more patience and faith to complete the puzzle and produce the desired outcome.

When I was a little girl growing up, my siblings and I were blessed to have a beautiful relationship with our

94

parents. I wanted so much to make my parents, especially my dad, proud of me. His face would light up when I showed him my good grades. I remember he and mom went with me to receive a scholarship where I had written an essay and won.

The essay was entitled, "Why Do I want to Go to College." I remember in the essay I expressed that I wanted all my life to go to college. It couldn't have been all my life but obviously they got the point as I wanted to make it a reality. That is what I wanted to do for my dad; I wanted to please him. I wanted to make him proud. In my own comprehension I believe I did.

I have come to see in my becoming that I just want to please God. I want Him to be proud of me. I want to do those things that are pleasing in His sight. I want to become what He desires me to be. Knowing that Jesus is the originator and the perfecter of my faith, I know I will.

Several years ago, the Lord led me to look up my middle name "Faye." This was interesting as I seldom use it if at all, although I often use my middle initial. When I looked up the name Faye, I found out that Faye means (in English, French, and Hebrew) "Confidence; trust; belief." It is a form of Faith. Maybe I will use my middle name more often. Could it be, I am ever evolving from Faye to Faith?

I have come to see and I believe that God is using me to share that you too are becoming. Your faith is becoming. Every time you exercise your faith by putting your trust in God, you are becoming. Even your reading this book is evidence of you becoming.

There was a time in your life that you lived without God, but now you have accepted Him into your heart. He wants our faith to grow. He wants our faith to produce. Your faith is getting stronger.

We are becoming what God desires us to be whether we immediately see the changes or not. God is masterful as He molds us each day more and more into His image.

When I was in college, I use to watch the late John Olsteen on TV. He would start each sermon with a pledge, "…This is my Bible, I am what it says I am, I can have what it says I can have…" That's welcoming faith into our lives. That is repeating God's promises over and over. That is becoming.

I have come to the resolve that finding God is finding Me. When we embrace God, we continue to evolve into Him. We become inseparable. When we embrace faith, we embrace God by having a conscious awareness of His presence in our lives. We cannot live without faith as we cannot live without God.

God knows our hearts and when our hearts are right, things will always work out. When I rest in God that He is doing a great work in me, and I believe in you also, we must know that everything about us is still evolving. Jesus has written the final script in our lives, but we must continue to look to Him as He perfects those things regarding us.

The puzzle is still being put together as we continue to evolve. I understand Paul when he said, "I count not myself to have apprehended but this one thing I do..." Paul understood that he had not arrived yet. He understood that he was ever evolving before he departed this life.

Ultimately, each day I am becoming all God desires me to be. My faith is ever increasing–I am ever evolving and so are you. My final faith script, your final faith script, is yet to be written. My dreams, your dreams, have not all been fulfilled. My life, your life, have not yet been perfected. We are ever evolving into what God has predestined us to be. We are continually evolving not on our terms, but, on God's terms as He is the finisher of our faith.

> "IF OUR FAITH IS ON TRIAL... BE ENCOURAGED THAT WE ARE JUST EVOLVING."

If our faith is on trial right now, meaning we are being tested, we should be encouraged that we are just evolving. We all are striving to get there where our trust is wholly dependent on God. Just like Abram evolved from Abram to Abraham, each day, I too, and prayerfully you are ever evolving from little faith to more faith to great faith.

Sandra F. Holt

My Prayer: *God open our hearts to see your hand in our lives. God, we want our faith to grow to ever evolve to total dependence on you. We truly want to do your will. May we see you in a greater way as we continue to go forward, as we continue to exercise our faith, and as we continue to grow in the nurture and admonition of you. May we continue to evolve to greater faith in Jesus' name! Amen.*

A Revised Letter to Faith,

Hello, Faith,

It is so wonderful that You are back in my life! With You being back in my life, I am truly convinced that nothing is impossible. In fact, Faith, I just wrote a book about You. I pray that many will read it so they can see what a wonderful difference you can make in their lives as you have made in mine. I am blessed beyond measure for your presence. Your unwavering support and protection mean the world to me now.

Sometimes words are even inadequate as I try to express the gladness you have reawaken in me. I want the readers to know that as well. I want the world to know it. In fact, each day, I stand in awe of you with utmost gratitude as I am so thankful that I need not worry about anymore hindrances and distractions because my complete trust in God will get me through any and every situation. I am so grateful that God has given You to me and I will never take You for granted again. I will use You as one of my major weapons to handle life's challenges. I see that we can accomplish so many awesome things together.

There are no limits in God, and I don't have to be concerned about time because You are NOW. Knowing You are a part of the armor of God that shields me from all the attacks of the enemy brings joy to my soul and spirit.

Faith, You came by hearing and hearing by the Word of God. You are priceless, and You make my life complete. What a beautiful journey we are on together. I truly believe there is so much more to see and accomplish as I connect with You through the power of our Al mighty God through Jesus Christ our Lord. I am already seeing amazing miracles as I utilize You.

Your absence in my life was felt, but no more! You are here to stay forever with me. I will not take another step in my life without You. No more restless nights hoping God will come through. No more added stress that creates turmoil in my body. No more lonely nights feeling sorry for myself. No more hoping things will work out. I now KNOW without any doubt that things will always work out. No more anxiety because You have taken care of every obstacle in my life.

I am ready to seize on all the promises God has for me because You will make sure it happens as I hold onto You. I am dreaming again and hoping again. It feels amazing. You truly make life good.

You are a powerful weapon in my spiritual life. I have seen so many victories since your return. As the song says, "I have seen too many victories to let defeat have the last word." Faith, You will always have the last word.

Also, Thank You for making sure Your enemies do

not touch me anymore. Wow! What an awesome life I am living, now, for you have truly rejuvenated me with your power. I look so forward to each day with You and take comfort in knowing I will never have to live with fear, doubt and unbelief again as you are constantly protecting me.

So, good night, Faith. I am about to end this letter and have another peaceful night because I know all is well in Jesus' name. I look forward to greeting You in the morning with,

"Hello Faith"

I EXTEND CHRIST TO YOU

Maybe after reading this book, you are now ready to accept Jesus Christ into your life. I extend the invitation to you. It only takes faith. John 3:16 says, "For God so loved the world, that he gave his only begotten Son, that whosever believeth in him should not perish, but have everlasting life."

Romans 10:9 states, "That if thou shalt confess with thou mouth the Lord Jesus, and shalt believe in thy heart that God has raised him from the dead, thou shalt be saved."

Please say this simple prayer: "Jesus, please come into my life. Please forgive me of my sins. I believe you are the Son of God and that you gave your life that I might be saved."

If you said this simple prayer and believe it, you are now part of the body of Christ.

WRITE YOUR LETTER TO FAITH

_____

_____

_____

_____

_____

_____

_____

_____

_____

_____

_____

_____

_____

_____

_____

_____

_____

_____

_____

_____

_____

_____

_____

WRITE YOUR LETTER TO FAITH

_____

_____

_____

_____

_____

_____

_____

_____

_____

_____

_____

_____

_____

_____

_____

_____

_____

_____

_____

_____

_____

www.ingramcontent.com/pod-product-compliance
Lightning Source LLC
Chambersburg PA
CBHW071025120626
46546CB00003B/1220